AN UNOFFICIAL ROBLOX BOOK

Ari
Avatar

MONSTER ESCAPE

First published by Scholastic in Australia, 2022
This edition published by Scholastic in the UK, 2022
1 London Bridge, London, SE1 9BG

Scholastic Ireland, 89E Lagan Road, Dublin Industrial Estate, Glasnevin, Dublin, D11 HP5F

Published by Scholastic Australia in 2022.
Text copyright © Scholastic Australia, 2022.
Illustrations copyright © Scholastic Australia, 2022.
Cover design by Hannah Janzen.
Internal design by Paul Hallam.

SCHOLASTIC and associated logos are trademarks and/or
registered trademarks of Scholastic Inc.

ISBN 978 0702 32873 2

A CIP catalogue record for this book is available from the British Library.

Printed in the UK by CPI Group UK (Ltd), Croydon, CR0 4YY

Paper made from wood grown in sustainable forests and other controlled sources.

1 3 5 7 9 10 8 6 4 2

www.scholastic.co.uk

MONDAY MORNING

I reached over and smacked my alarm so it would stop blaring in my ear. I was having an awesome dream that I had been sucked into a portal and I'd come out in another world where I was a **MILLIONAIRE TYCOON. YESSSS!** Being a tycoon would be so cool. **FREE ROBUX** for all my friends! Massive adventure—

'Ari Avatar, get up now!' a voice boomed from the doorway.

I didn't need to look up. I knew it was my mum.

'You need to be at school in thirty minutes. **GET UP!'** she hollered.

I groaned. But as
I tried to pull the
blanket over my
head, I suddenly
felt something wet
on my face. Not

just wet. Drippy, slobbery wet.

'Coda.' I tried to push my pet dog
away, but her tongue only licked
faster. 'OK, OK, I'm getting up,'
I said, sitting up straight in my
bed. I knew when I was bloxxed.
There was no winning against the
SLOBBER NINJA.

Coda smiled at me and I caved.

Coda is my dog. We adopted her last year from the nursery. The guy there gave me a **COOL EGG** and I took care of it. Finally, it hatched and out came Coda! And she loves me the most because I took care of her egg.

I crawled out of bed and limped down the stairs. My legs were still sore from playing on Zeke's latest **OBBY** in his backyard. His dad builds obstacle courses for the Avatar Army, and sometimes he creates mini obbies in their garden to test them out. Zeke and I had been playing on it all weekend and now my legs felt like jelly.

'Morning, sleepy,' Mum said as I
sat down at the table. I groaned
at her as I poured my cereal into
the bowl.

'Morning!' a high-pitched voice
squealed.

I winced as my younger sister
came bounding into the kitchen.
My sister, AKA the most
ANNOYING AVATAR
you have ever met in your life.
Like, seriously. She listens to the
most annoying music and sings

so loud. She has her annoying friends over and they try to play tricks on me. Like the time they put lipstick on me while I was asleep and I rushed off to my football game with it still on my face the next day.

'Morning, Ally,' Mum said, giving her a kiss.

CRINGE.

When Mum turned her back, Ally poked her tongue out at me. I rolled my eyes.

'Eat up, Ari, I want to see you out the door and on the bus before I leave for the party-supply shop,' Mum said. Mum's a party planner. I know that sounds cool—like we have loads of parties in our house or something—but it's not those kinds of parties. It's more like boring weddings or adult dinner parties. I mean, don't get me wrong, my mum is pretty good at her job. But it's not the kind of party I'd want to go to.

'MORNING, BLOCKHEADS!' Dad sang as he rushed into the kitchen.

'Morning,' Ally chirped.

'You'd better hurry or you'll be late,' Dad said, looking at me in my pyjamas. 'It's almost eight o'block!'

I stared at him.

'Get it? Eight *o'block?*'

Dad joke. **TOTALLY LAME.** I scooped up the last mouthfuls of cereal, hurried back to my room and changed into my clothes from the day before. Mum would probably notice, but I didn't have time to find anything else.

I picked up my schoolbag, flung it over my shoulder and flew down the stairs. Only one minute to go before the bus got here.

I ran through the kitchen, scooping up my lunch and throwing it into my bag.

'Hey, are you wearing yesterday's—' Mum began, but I cut her off.

'Can't talk, gotta go!' I yelled over my shoulder, running out the front door.

As I got to the end of my street,

I saw that the bus was already there. I did a **SAFETY VAULT** over the bench and rolled straight through the bus doors just before they closed. **EZ.**

'Just made it, Ari,' the bus driver said, shaking her head as I climbed aboard.

I could see my sister, Ally, in the front row of the bus with her friend, whispering and laughing. Ally pointed at me and laughed again.

'You're such a **NOOB**,' I said.

As I walked up the aisle of the bus, I noticed others giggling at me. What was going on?

At the back of the bus, my best friend, Zeke, was sitting, looking out the window. As I approached him, he coughed and then **LAUGHED,** which made his block face go all red.

'Your pants aren't done up,' he said, nodding down at my trousers.

'UGH!'

I quickly zipped up my trousers.

'You're such a **BLOCKHEAD,'**
he laughed.

I punched him playfully in the
arm. But I wasn't really angry.
Zeke and I had been **BEST**

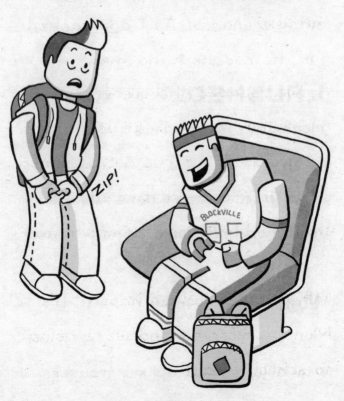

ZIP!

AVATARS since we were like, four years old.

The bus ambled up the main street of Blockville, stopping to collect more avatars along the way.

As we rounded the corner, I saw a familiar face look at us through the window. The bus doors opened and our friend Jez rushed onto the bus. She looked super excited.

'Why do you look so happy? It's Monday morning and we're going to school,' I said.

Jez sat down and opened her backpack. She pulled out her tablet and flicked it on.

'I think I've found a **PORTAL,**' she said.

Zeke and I rolled our eyes. Jez is a complete computer pro. She can hack into just about anything, including the army systems that tracked portals, which apparently sometimes opened up in Blockville. They

16

reckon they lead to **OTHER BLOCK WORLDS,** but nobody I know had ever seen one. I wasn't even sure they existed. Jez was obsessed with tracking them through the army database.

'You're never going to find one,' Zeke said. 'My dad tracks them all the time for his job, and he says they **DISAPPEAR** faster than you can track them.'

'My dad says they're fake,' I said.

Zeke frowned.

Jez shrugged, not looking worried at all. 'I'll get it one day.'

I couldn't help but smile at Jez. We'd been friends since the third grade, and if there was one thing I knew about Jez, it was that once she'd put her mind to something, she usually got it done. She was cool like that.

The bus pulled up outside our school. There was a huge sign saying, 'Blockville School—creating the best students on the block.' I **CRINGED** every time I read it.

We stepped off the bus out the front of the school just as the bell rang out.

'MOVE IT, NOOBS!' someone said as they pushed past us, sending the three of us stumbling into the garden.

'Watch it, Trip,' Jez yelled at Trip and his two friends, who had run off ahead.

Trip was the most annoying avatar in the school. He thought he **OWNED** the place, just because his mum was the mayor of Blockville. He also thought he was a total pro at everything.

We entered the school hallway and split off to go to our separate classes.

'See ya at lunch!' Zeke called.

I pulled my bag up my shoulder and jogged on to class.

MONDAY
LUNCHTIME

'That was the most **BORING** lesson ever,' I said, sitting down at the table with Zeke and Jez.

'I thought it was awesome,' Jez said. 'I've almost finished coding a whole new backyard for my house!'

'Only you would love Code class,' Zeke said, throwing a grape at her.

Jez rolled her eyes. 'One day my computer skills are going to **SAVE YOUR BUTTS** and then you won't be so smug.'

'Yeah right,' I laughed.

Jez smiled. She knew we were just messing with her.

'I got a new record on the obby,' Zeke said, his eyes lighting up. 'Eight minutes and thirty-six seconds.'

'Wow,' I said. 'Total **PRO.**'

Zeke is a machine. He can get through any obby in record time. He is so strong and fast.

'Who's a pro?' a voice said from behind me.

'I told you this morning, get lost, Trip,' Jez said.

Trip and his two blockhead friends, Levi and Elle, shoved us up the bench as they joined us at our table.

'What do you blockheads want?' I said.

'I just heard you talking about someone being a pro, so I figured you must be talking about me,' Trip said, smirking.

Levi and Elle laughed. They only laughed because they were copying Trip. They were always copying Trip. They even tried to wear their hair the same way as him. **SO LAME.**

'No, we were talking about how Zeke is the **BIGGEST OBBY PRO** you've ever seen,' I said.

'Is that right?' Trip said.

'Yeah, it is,' I said. 'And Jez here is the **QUEEN OF TECH—** she could code you right out of existence if she wanted to!'

'So, what can *you* do, then?' Trip said, pointing his block hand at me.

'I . . . I can . . .' I stammered.

Trip laughed loudly. Then Elle and Levi copied, laughing even louder. Trip stopped laughing, but Elle and Levi didn't notice and kept snorting until Trip elbowed them sharply.

'What?!' they said in unison.

'Ari is **BRAVE,**' Jez interrupted Trip's friends.

I sat up straighter.

'Yeah, Ari is **THE BRAVEST**

AVATAR I know,' Zeke added.

I smiled. It was good to have mates like these avatars.

'Brave, huh?' Trip said. 'I've never seen you do anything brave.'

'I am brave,' I said. But I didn't feel confident anymore.

'If you're so brave, how about a **DARE?**' Trip said.

'What kind of dare?' I asked, unsure.

'I dunno,' Trip said, thinking.

'Something other people are
scared of.'

'Ari will do your dare!' Jez yelled.

Wait, what?

'Yeah, he'll crush your dare!'
Zeke added.

Please stop.

'OK, then,' Trip said, an **EVIL**
smile on his face. 'Meet me after
school, at the industrial compound
on the edge of town.'

'I think I'm busy—' I started.

"YOU'RE ON!" Jez and Zeke
said in chorus.

Trip and his blockhead friends
stood up and walked off,
whispering and laughing.

'Are you avatars insane?!' I yelled
once Trip had left.

'What?' Jez asked.

I frowned. I did want to look
brave, but I also knew I shouldn't
have to prove myself to a

blockhead like Trip. And there was no way I wanted to go to the edge of town to an abandoned building.

'I don't want to do some dare in the industrial compound at the edge of town! That place is **CREEPY!**' I said.

'But don't you want to show that noob who is the real pro?' Zeke asked.

I bit my lip. Did I really need to show Trip? And was it too late to back out now?

MONDAY
AFTER
SCHOOL

We caught the bus to the outskirts of Blockville to the compound with abandoned warehouses.

'I really don't like this place. It's so **SPOOKY**,' I said, as we climbed the fence into the area.

The ground was dusty and several worn-out buildings towered over us. Most of them had broken windows, paint peeling and even big holes in the walls, as if someone had blown the side right off the building with explosives.

'Where's Trip?' Zeke asked.

Jez and I shrugged and decided we should walk around and look for him.

There were old tyres, rusty barrels and even a burnt-out car  sitting in the compound.

It was like a **ZOMBIE**
apocalypse had happened and
we were the only avatars left in
the world.

A cool breeze blew, and kicked
up the dust around our feet.
I coughed.

'Maybe he's in this old building,'
I said, standing on my tippy-toes
to look into one of the windows.

Zeke jumped up and hung off
the windowsill. He then did a
chin-up and looked inside.

Chin-ups were the easiest thing
in the world for Zeke.

'Anything?' Jez called from below.

'**NOTHING,**' Zeke said.

We decided to try the next building.

We walked slowly around the
compound, looking into the
abandoned warehouses on the
way. But Trip and the blockheads
were nowhere to be found.

'What about that building down
there?' Jez said, pointing to a

lone building at the base of the compound.

It was the **SCARIEST** of all the buildings. The shattered windows were boarded up with wood panels. The walls were rusty and the building had a really **WEIRD** vibe.

'BOOO!'

'AAAGGGH!'

'Hahaha, look at your faces!' Trip taunted. He and the blockheads had just jumped out of a barrel that was standing outside the warehouse.

'Trip, you blockhead!' Zeke yelled.

Trip cackled harder.

'So, what's with the **FREAKY** warehouse?' Jez said, trying to change the subject.

'That's your dare,' Trip said. 'Ari, you have to go inside and bring something out.'

'That's not even hard,' I scoffed. I hoped they didn't hear the tremor in my voice.

'Oh, but I forgot to tell you about
the **MONSTER** that lives
there,' Trip said with a sinister smile.

'Monster?' I stammered.

'Yeah, everyone knows about the
monster,' Levi said.

'The monster turns intruders into
STATUES,' Elle added.

Zeke, Jez and I exchanged glances.

'That's not true,' Jez said.

'You sure about that?' Trip teased.

I looked up at the old building.
In one of the shattered windows
on the top floor, I thought I saw
something move. I swallowed hard.

'Do you want me to come?'
Zeke asked.

I shook my head. I wanted to show
Trip I could be brave. Zeke was
the obby king. Jez was the tech
queen. I had to be . . . something.

I silently crept into the entrance
of the building. The door had

been removed at some stage,
so it wasn't hard to get in.

Inside, the room had concrete
floors and concrete walls. There
were exposed pipes running along
the ceiling and a metal staircase
that led to another level. It was
pretty dark in there and I couldn't
see too far in. But there was
a **RUMBLING** noise that
sounded like it was coming
from upstairs.

I took one step forward, and
started shivering. It was really
cold in the warehouse.

My legs started to **SHAKE** slightly as I stalked forward, one foot in front of the other.

Just get an item and get out of here, I told myself.

CLANG!

My eyes darted upwards.

Something was **MOVING** at the top of the stairs!

I held my breath.

Silence.

I took another few steps forward.
I could just make out a doorway
into another room. There was
nothing to take out of the main
entryway, so I thought I'd try my
luck in the next room.

I cautiously entered the room.
There was a bit of sunlight
coming through the boarded-up
windows, and I could see what
was in here.

'Whoa,' I mumbled.

There was a computer sitting on a
table. And it was glowing brightly.

How can a computer be working in an abandoned building?

CLANG!

I jumped at the sound.

'Who . . . who's there?' I stammered.

I heard footsteps.

BOOM. BOOM. BOOM.

I looked wildly around the room.
There was no escape other than

the door I came in through. I took
a step backwards.

'RAAAAAARGH!' a shadowy figure
in the doorway hollered.

'AAAAGH!' I pushed past the
creature and ran for my life. I
burst out of the warehouse and
into the sunshine which stabbed
at my eyes.

'RUN—THE MONSTER!'
I yelled.

Trip laughed loudly.

'No, for real,' I said. 'I saw it!'

Jez and Zeke looked confused.

I turned around and saw the
figure in the entrance to the
warehouse. It looked like someone
covered in an dirty old blanket.

The blanket was thrown to the
ground and underneath were Elle
and Levi, laughing and pointing
at me.

REEEEEEEE!

'You blockheads!' I said, kicking the

gravel. 'What a dirty trick.'

'Looks like I win the dare,'
Trip cackled.

'No way, that was **UNFAIR!**'
I protested.

'**REPLAY!**' demanded Zeke.

'OK, OK,' Trip said. 'I'll give you
one more chance.'

Trip was interrupted by his watch
beeping. 'Oh man, it's my mum.
I'm busted.'

'But what about my second chance?' I said. I wanted to have another go at the warehouse. I wanted to prove I could do it.

'I've gotta go,' Trip said. 'But I'll meet you here tomorrow after school again. And it's your **LAST CHANCE.'**

Trip, Elle and Levi ran off, kicking up the dust as they went.

'That was totally unfair,' Jez said.

'Yeah, sorry, Ari,' Zeke added. 'Levi and Elle said they were

leaving—we didn't realise
they'd gone into the warehouse
to scare you.'

'It's OK, I'll do it tomorrow,' I said.

'Let's get out of here—this place
is **WEIRD,**' Jez said.

As we turned to leave, I looked up
at one of the windows that wasn't
boarded up.
A **SHADOW**
hovered by
the window
and then
disappeared.

MONDAY NIGHT

I lay in bed, staring at the ceiling.
I couldn't stop thinking about
what happened at the compound. I
wanted to go back, but I was also
a little **FREAKED OUT.**
It was totally strange that there
was a computer in the warehouse.
And it was on. That had to mean
that somebody had been in there.
And I was sure that I saw a
shadow in the top window.

I shuddered. I definitely didn't

want to see that again.

But then I thought harder. What kind of **RANDO** would set up their computer in an abandoned warehouse? It couldn't actually have been a monster, right? That sounded like a silly kids' story.

I drifted off to sleep and dreamed of old buildings and hairy monsters.

TUESDAY LUNCHTIME

'What are you avatars doing this weekend?' Zeke asked.

'I want to go to the **TECH MALL** and get this cool new hard drive,' Jez said. 'Didn't you want to get that new surfboard, Zeke?'

'I'm out of Robux,' Zeke said sadly. 'Dad said I need to earn them by doing chores before I can get the board.'

'Boring,' Jez said.

'Why don't you come help me work for my mum?' I asked. 'She always needs help making party bags and things like that for her party-planning business. Not the best fun, but she pays good Robux.'

'That'd be cool!' Zeke said. 'Beats washing my dad's car. Want to come over and test the **OBBY** with me again? You too, Jez,' Zeke said.

'Sure,' I answered. 'What has your dad created this time?'

'It's a maze. The real thing is going to be epic. We have the mini maze in our backyard and even though it's just a prototype, it's **TOTALLY AWESOME,**' Zeke said.

'Man, it'd be so cool to have a dad who is an obby designer,' I said.

'Most of the time,' Zeke said. 'Except for that time when Dad designed an obby maze so hard that my brother got lost in there for two days!'

'**OOF!**' I said.

'How are you feeling about the dare this afternoon?' Jez asked.

'OK, I guess.'

'You'll be fine,' Zeke said. 'We can come in with you this time.'

I thought for a moment. I didn't want to look like a **TOTAL NOOB** who was too scared to do the dare alone. 'I dunno . . .'

'Not to shadow you,' Jez added. 'Just to keep a lookout and make

sure Trip and his blockhead
friends don't try to pull another
prank on you.'

It would be good knowing my
friends were with me, I figured.
And if there was some kind
of trouble in the warehouse,
it wouldn't be all bad having
an **OBBY PRO** and a
HACKER with me.

We finished up our lunch and the
bell rang.

'What have you got on now?'
Zeke asked.

'Coding, yay!' Jez cheered.

I rolled my eyes. 'I've got Economics,'
I said.

I glanced up and saw Trip
walking into the school building. He
turned and smirked at me.

Jez saw me looking at Trip. 'Don't
worry, you'll show him,' she said.

I hoped so.

TUESDAY AFTERNOON

We climbed the rickety fence
of the compound at the edge
of town. The sky was filled with
clouds and there was a cold wind,
which made it feel about ten times
CREEPIER than the day
before. We headed straight for
the abandoned warehouse and
saw Trip waiting.

'Where are the blockheads?'
Jez teased.

'Levi and Elle couldn't come,' Trip said. 'But that's OK. It's my dare.'

'So, I just have to grab something from the warehouse?' I said. **'EZ.** Even a noob could do that.'

'Uh-uh. You have to grab something from the **TOP FLOOR,**' Trip said.

'Hey, that wasn't part of the dare,' Jez said.

'Yeah, but he's already had one chance. The dare gets harder each day,' Trip said.

'Who says?' Zeke said.

'I say. And this is how it's gonna work. I'm going to come into the entrance with you so I can check you aren't cheating. I want to see you go up those stairs, right past **THE MONSTER,** and bring something down. And I'm going to watch that your friends don't do it for you,' Trip said.

'Fine. I can do that. I'm a **PRO** at this stuff,' I said, standing up straighter. I sure hoped Trip didn't hear the **WOBBLE** in my voice.

I led the way to the open entrance and walked inside. The lobby was so cold and dim, it was like **DANGER CENTRAL.** We moved slowly, our feet scuffing against the concrete floor.

'We'll wait here,' Trip said as we reached the bottom of the metal staircase. 'You go up.'

I swallowed hard.

'Bring proof,' he said.

Jez and Zeke nodded at me in encouragement.

You can do this, I told myself as I put my foot on the first rung of the steps. It made a slight clanging sound against the hard industrial metal.

Did something just shift on the floor above me? I turned to look at the others.

'CHICKEN?' Trip taunted.

I spun around and stepped up another rung. **'EZ,'** I said.

Suddenly, there was an almighty **CLUNK** behind us. A huge metal

door dropped down and the
sound reverberated around the
warehouse as it hit the ground.

'Wait! Since when is there a door
on the entrance?!' Zeke said.

'It dropped down from above,' Jez
said. 'We didn't see it before!'

We all ran to the metal door
that was blocking our escape.
We pounded on it to see if we
could shift it, but the metallic
thud bounced around the room.
It sounded like the **DRUMS
OF DOOM.**

'This door feels a million blocks thick!' Trip said. I could see he looked scared now. 'What do we do?'

'There's no handle,' I said, feeling along the doorframe. There was a button that **GLOWED RED.** I banged it, but it didn't do anything.

'It's computer controlled,' Jez said, leaning in and running her hand along some kind of electronic control pad.

'Looks like it needs to scan something to open. That or we hack our way out through the main system. But there's no way there are computers in here.'

'There are!' I yelled, suddenly remembering the computer I saw. All eyes turned to me in surprise. 'I saw it yesterday. It was over here,' I said, pointing to the room on the opposite side of the hall.

Just as we were about to move, we heard a loud **THUMPING** noise.

'That sounds like . . .' Zeke began.

'Footsteps,' Jez whispered.

My friends' eyes were super wide with fear.

Then we heard it.

A huge, loud,

'ROOOOOOAAAAARRR!'

TUESDAY AFTERNOON — A BIT LATER

'Hide!' Jez squeaked.

We searched **DESPERATELY** for a place to hide. From the entrance room, we could see narrow passages extending off in different directions. And in front of us was a flight of metal stairs. The **THUMPING** seemed to be coming from above, so I didn't want to take my chances going up. But the narrow passageways looked **CONFUSING.** I didn't want to get lost in there either.

There was a **CREAKING** noise above us. We looked up.

'AAAAAAGH!'

We could see to the next level, and there behind the barricade

was a huge figure. He was a
MASSIVE avatar covered
in **THICK HAIR,** and in
his hand he held a club. His red
beady eyes glared down at us.

'MONSTER!' we all yelled
in unison.

We had no choice. We ran up
the corridor to our left, hoping it
wasn't going to be a dead end.
There were rooms which broke off
the corridor, but as we glanced in
each one, there didn't seem to be
anywhere to hide inside. We didn't
want to get cornered in a room.

'How are we going to get out of here?!' Trip whimpered.

'It's like I said,' Jez panted. 'The door is controlled by the computer. We just need to **FIND THE COMPUTER** and then I can hack us out.'

The monster's footsteps got louder. We needed to move—**NOW!**

As we ran further up the corridor, I could just make out what was ahead. My stomach lurched. It was a wall. **A DEAD END.**

We hit the wall at speed and banged on it.

'What do we do?' Zeke gasped.

I looked around anxiously for a doorway or ceiling vent.

'There!' I said, as my eyes lowered to the ground.

Next to us, at the bottom of the wall, was **A VENT.** I ripped off the metal covering and beckoned the others to follow. 'The monster won't fit through here!' I said.

I shimmied through the hole and was followed by Zeke and Jez. But there was no sign of Trip.

'Where's Trip?' Jez said with wide eyes.

We cautiously peered back through the vent, only to witness the monster pointing his club at a terrified-looking Trip. Trip covered his eyes as a **BOLT OF LIGHT** zapped out of the end of the club.

Jez screamed.

In that moment, Trip turned into a
STATUE.

The monster gave a bellowing
laugh and reached out to grab
the stone version of Trip. He
dragged Trip behind him, moving
back up the corridor.

'Trip's a statue!' Zeke exclaimed,
shaking his head. 'I can't believe
the stories are true!'

'What was that thing he used to
turn Trip into stone?' I asked.

'I've read about these,' Jez said. 'They're clubs from another **PORTAL** that can turn things to stone. But they're a type of software, not magic. If we can get to the computer, I can turn Trip back *and* hack open the exit. We just have to find that computer.'

There were more narrow corridors stretching out ahead of us. And there were several rooms branching off.

'We'll just have to check every room,' I said.

'We'd better hurry,' Zeke said. 'Once the monster has taken Trip to wherever he keeps his statue collection, I reckon he'll be back for us.'

'I think you're right. **LET'S GO!**' Jez said.

I led the way. We jogged up the corridor, puffing breathlessly. Each time we saw a room, we ducked our heads inside before moving on. All the rooms seemed to be empty.

We rounded a corner and suddenly found ourselves back

in the main entrance where we'd come in earlier.

'WHICH WAY?' Jez asked desperately.

'I know there was a computer down that way,' I said, pointing to another corridor. 'But I also heard the monster going back up these metal stairs. He'll have Trip with him for sure.'

'So, which way?' Zeke asked.

'Let's get Trip first,' Jez said.

We ran to the big, black, metal staircase. I put one foot on it, and it made a light clanging sound.

We'd need to tiptoe. I gently padded up the stairs, holding on to the rail to try to lighten my weight. Jez and Zeke followed.

When we got to the top of the stairs, we saw more corridors. There was a **BRIGHT RED GLOW** coming from further up the hall. It had to be where Trip was, I was sure of it.

TUESDAY AFTERNOON — EVEN LATER

When we reached the room with the glow, we slowed to a stop and hid behind the doorway wall. I carefully twisted my head to look into the room. But there was **NO SIGN** of the monster. I waved Jez and Zeke to follow me.

Once inside, we could see what was causing the red glow. It was a big **GLASS CASE.**

And it was holding Trip, who was as frozen as a statue.

'Trip!' Zeke yelled.

'Shhh!' Jez hissed.

We ran over to the case.

'Is he . . . dead?' Zeke asked.

Jez shook her head as she looked over an **ELECTRONIC PANEL** on the side of the glass cage. It **BEEPED** and little red-and-yellow buttons flashed.

'He's not dead. This is the computer life monitor. I can tell he's alive.'

'But will he be stone **FOREVER?'** I said, my voice shaking.

'No, he will only remain frozen in stone if he stays in here. If we can **HACK** this case open, he'll unfreeze,' Jez said.

'Well, do your hacky thing, then!' Zeke said urgently.

Jez rolled her eyes. 'I need to find

the computer that is powering this thing. Once we find it, I can hack this network as well as the exits. Then we can get Trip and get the heck out of here.'

It sounded like a plan.

'Ari, where was the computer?' Jez said.

'Downstairs, along that first corridor,' I said.

'Are you sure?' Zeke asked.

I nodded. 'Totally. **LET'S GO!**'

We ran out of the room and back to the metal staircase. We tiptoed down, one by one, trying not to make a sound as our shoes made contact with each metallic step. When we got to the bottom, I silently pointed to the right corridor—the one I had been down the day before.

We jogged on our toes up the hall and turned into the room. There in front of us was a **GLOWING COMPUTER** on a stand.

'I was right!' I said excitedly.

'Good job, pro.' Jez winked.

I beamed.

We ran up to the computer
and Jez hit the keyboard, which
brought up a screen. To me, it
looked like a complicated line of
code that I didn't understand
at all.

'I wish I'd paid more attention in
Coding class,' Zeke whispered.

I nodded. Me too.

But Jez was all over it. She was

a **TOTAL HACKING PRO!**

Her fingers danced over the keyboard, adding in lines of code and deleting old lines. She frowned and squinted as she navigated the screens, minimising one then bringing up another.

'Do you want the good news or the **BAD NEWS?**' she finally said, turning to face us.

'The good news?' I suggested.

'I can open the exits from this computer. It won't take me long—like, maybe five minutes,' she said.

'Then what's the bad news?' Zeke asked.

'This computer isn't controlling the glass case that Trip is in. I can't hack him out from here.'

OOF.

'Let's just get out of here,'
Zeke said, bouncing up and
down nervously.

'We can't **LEAVE TRIP!**'
I said.

'Why not? He's a **TOTAL**
blockhead,' Zeke said.

'He may be a blockhead, but he
doesn't deserve to live like a
statue,' I said.

'We can get help and come back.'

Zeke's eyes were like big, round saucers, pleading with me.

'Who knows what the monster will have done with him by then,' I said.

Zeke and I looked at Jez.

Jez opened her mouth and then slowly said, 'I'm with Ari. We need to **RESCUE TRIP.**'

Zeke rolled his eyes.

'I can hack open the exit first and you can get out if you want,'

Jez said to Zeke.

Zeke let out a puff of air.
'Nah, we're a team. We do this
TOGETHER.'

I smiled at my friend.

'Let's find this other computer,
then!' I said, high-fiving Jez
and Zeke.

But then we heard it. Loud,
thumping **FOOTSTEPS.**

TUESDAY AFTERNOON— A LOT LATER

Our heads whipped up as we looked at each other with wild eyes. The monster was coming.

'What do we do?' breathed Zeke.

'We need to find that other computer to free Trip,' Jez said.

The footsteps grew **LOUDER.**

Suddenly, **A HUGE FIGURE**

filled the doorway. It was covered in dark hair and its red eyes flashed. It held up its club and pointed it at us as it let out a mighty . . .

'ROOOOOOAAARRR!'

'AAAAAAAGGGH!' we screamed.

I looked around the room. 'There!' I yelled, pointing to another vent on the bottom of the wall.

We dived to the ground and I ripped the grate off the wall. We scurried through the small

hole—first Zeke, then Jez. I
pushed myself through the hole
just as the monster's heavy
footsteps **THUDDED** behind me. I
felt a rush of air as the monster
GRABBED for my leg. I
whipped my legs through the
vent, just in time.

The footsteps thundered away from us.

'Phew,' said Zeke.

'We won't have long,' Jez said, starting to jog out of the new room we were in. 'That monster knows his home inside out. I'm sure he's just going around, ready to meet us on the other side. **LET'S GET MOVING.'**

We raced up the corridor, checking each room for a new computer. We also listened for the monster's footsteps.

When we reached the end of the
next corridor, it opened out into
the main lobby again.

'Right, which corridor haven't we
taken yet?' Jez asked.

I pointed to the one that ran
behind the metal stairs. 'That way!'

We bolted up the corridor, our
feet pounding the cold concrete
floor. Each time we reached a new
room, we'd stick our heads inside
to see if there was a computer.

No luck.

As we reached the end of the corridor, we saw there was one room left. We turned into it, and there, inside, was a computer sitting on a stand.

Jez ran up to it and pressed some of the keys. The computer hummed to life. She tapped away **FRANTICALLY** at the keyboard, pulling up different lines of code.

'This is it!' she said excitedly. 'I just need **FIVE MINUTES** to hack into the security system and then I can free Trip.'

We heard the ominous **THUD** of footsteps.

'I'll never get it done in time,' Jez said, looking up at us with wide eyes.

'We need to distract the monster,' I said firmly to Zeke. 'You're fast and I'm smart. I reckon we can beat him.'

Zeke hesitated, then nodded. 'Let's do this,' he said.

TUESDAY AFTERNOON — MUCH LATER

Zeke and I ran out into the corridor, just in time to see the monster rounding the corner. He **ROARED** as he pointed his club in our direction.

'Come and get us!' Zeke yelled.

He then **DIVED** to the ground and pulled another grate off a vent and we scuttled through. The vent spat us out into the main lobby again.

We could hear the angry roar of the monster as he ran back down the corridor, trying to find us.

'Let's go up,' I said, pointing at the central metal staircase.

Zeke nodded.

We thundered up the staircase as we heard the monster **BURST** into the lobby. He **STOMPED** up the stairs, chasing us onto the next level.

'Do we outrun him or hide?' I asked desperately.

'I can outrun him any day. You should hide then get to Trip,' Zeke said quickly.

Ahead of me, I saw a cupboard with its door ajar. I ran up to it and slipped inside. I shut the door behind me, but left a **TINY CRACK** open so I could see what was happening.

I could no longer see Zeke, but I did see the monster reach the top of the stairs. He **SNIFFED** the air and started stalking up the corridor towards me.

My heart began **POUNDING** like crazy. *Why did I hide?* Now I was trapped.

He came closer and closer. Then he reached out his hairy arm towards the door. I was **DOOMED!**

'Hey, you big, **HAIRY BEAST,** I bet you can't catch me!' Zeke's voice echoed from the outside of the cupboard.

The monster whipped around to face him.

Zeke, RUN, I screamed inside my own head.

I could just see Zeke through the crack in the doorway. He was too close to the monster. There was no way he could **ESCAPE** and run down the stairs without being caught. What was he thinking?!

The monster gained speed and reached out to **GRAB** Zeke. But just as he was about to get him, Zeke was **VAULTING** over the barricade and then flying down to the level below.

'OOF!' I heard him say as he landed.

For a second I thought Zeke was a goner, but then I remembered, Zeke was the obby pro! He was a **PARKOUR NINJA** and I'd seen him jump off heights like that a million times before! He knew how to land softly and roll so that his body absorbed the impact. Sure enough, I could hear his footsteps running away on the level below.

Zeke was a **PRO!**

The monster **SCREAMED** in frustration and bounded down the stairs, looking for Zeke.

I quietly crept out of the cupboard and ran up the corridor that led to Trip. I just hoped that Zeke could keep the monster busy while Jez finished hacking and I freed Trip.

I ran as fast as I could up the corridor that led to the glass cabinet where Trip was captured. I **BURST** into the room and saw him, still frozen. Running to the case, I pounded on the side. It was still locked shut and glowing red. Jez hadn't hacked it yet.

I looked around frantically.

'Come on, Jez, you can do it,' I whispered.

I heard the **FOOTSTEPS** of the monster again. But this time, he was heading straight towards me.

TUESDAY AFTERNOON— EVEN LATER STILL

Come on, Jez, I thought again.

I hit the button to open the case and it **BEEPED** like an error message.

The footsteps grew **LOUDER.**

Come on, Jez!

Suddenly, the whole case changed from red to blue. I could see that

Trip's stiff arms began to move. Slowly, his body became soft again and he crumpled to the floor.

'Trip!' I yelled.

I **DIVED** forward and hit the glowing blue button. It sang a happy chime and the glass door on the case **WHOOSHED** open.

'Wha-what happened?' Trip stammered, standing up and rubbing his head.

'The monster turned you into a statue. But there's no time

to explain. He's **COMING BACK** and we need to get out of here!'

Trip's face was full of fear. 'I . . . I can't!' he said shakily.

'Yes, you can. I'll help you,' I said, putting my hand on his arm. 'You've got this.'

Trip looked at my hand then up to my face. I nodded and smiled. Then Trip smiled back. **'LET'S DO THIS,'** he said firmly.

At that moment, the monster

BURST into the room.

'What do we do?' Trip screamed.

'Look for a vent!' I yelled.

'There!' Trip said, pointing across the room.

The monster had learned our tricks and eyed the vent too. Would we make it across the room before he did?

We ran as fast as we could and dived to the ground. I **RIPPED** the grate open and

pushed Trip through first. Then
I **SHIMMIED** my body
through the hole.

The monster
**ROARED WITH
ANGER.**

'We need to meet
Jez at the other computer while
she hacks us through the exit,'
I said.

'How . . . how did you get me out?'
Trip asked.

'Jez hacked you out,' I told him.

'Jez hacked me out?' Trip said, surprised.

'Of course she did. She's only, like, the most pro hacker in our entire school. You'd know if you weren't so busy being mean to her all the time,' I said.

For a second, Trip looked a bit **GUILTY.**

'Come on,' I said.

TUESDAY, ALMOST SUNSET

Trip and I thundered down the stairs. We didn't have much time before the monster would **CATCH UP** to us. I remembered which corridor led to the exit computer and I ran into the room. Jez was startled.

'You scared me!' Jez yelled, then turned back to the computer. 'The problem with hacking is that the monster will definitely know that I'm on this computer,' she breathed.

'His tech will alert him to it. So we need to act **FAST.**'

'Where's Zeke?' I asked, worried.

'I haven't seen him since you two ran away to distract the monster,' Jez said.

Trip and I looked at each other with worried faces.

The computer made a loud noise. **DUNNN!**

'What does that mean?' I asked.

'It means I got the hack **WRONG,**' Jez said while trying a new code combination.

The computer made another loud error noise. **DUNNN!**

'How many shots do you get at this?' Trip asked Jez.

Jez looked up slowly. 'Well, each system is different. But most often it's usually around . . . **THREE.**'

'Three?!' Trip yelled. 'You've just used up two!'

'Yeah I did, so you'd better
BACK OFF so I can
concentrate on my last attempt!'
Jez yelled at him.

Trip backed off and stood
with me by the door, listening
for the monster.

'I think I know what I did wrong,'
Jez said, tapping the keys
furiously. 'I know what I can try.'

'Wait, what's that?' Trip said,
looking up.

Sure enough, the **THUNDERING**

footsteps of the monster sounded
as he thumped down the stairs.

'He's coming!' Trip said. 'Hack faster!'

Jez's fingers were a blur, they
were moving so fast.

The footsteps got **LOUDER.**

Jez was a typing machine. If typing
was a brick battle, Jez would've
bloxxed every player by now!

The footsteps got **LOUDER.**
We could see the monster at
the top of the corridor. His red

eyes met ours and he gave us a
MENACING frown.

'He's coming!' I yelled.

As he **STOMPED** up the hallway,
roaring as he went, I heard Jez
type one more furious line of code.
Trip and I ran over to her.

'It's now or never,' Jez said,
exhaling.

The monster burst into the room
and pointed his club at us.

Jez hit the final key.

'**BLIIIING!**' the computer chimed.

'Got it!' Jez yelled.

We **DIVED** down to the vent next to the computer and scurried through. Once we got to the other side, we breathed deeply.

'That was close,' I said.

'Come on,' Jez said. 'Let's get back to the main entrance. I can open the door from there.'

'But what about Zeke?!' I said.

'Let's hope we find him on the way!'

We ran up the corridor and burst out into the lobby, sprinting for the exit. But just as we were about to get to the door, something huge and hairy dropped down from the level above us.

'**AAAAAAAGGGH!**' we all screamed at once.

The monster was **BLOCKING** our exit. What could we do?

He breathed heavily, slobbering as he caught his breath. Up close, I could see he was taller than any avatar I'd ever seen. He **GROWLED** menacingly.

'What now?' Trip whispered.

'Look!' I yelled, as a ball of avatar came flying down from the level above.

It was Zeke! He had done a **JUMP SPIN** from the upper level and was flying downwards towards the monster. The monster looked up and lifted his club to shoot Zeke into a statue.

'NOOOO!' I yelled. I dropped

to the ground and rolled into the
monster's feet.

The club went **FLYING** out of
the monster's hands, into the air.

Zeke **COLLIDED**
with the monster,
knocking him to
the ground.

As the club came hurtling downwards, it released a beam of light.

ZAAAAAP!

The beam collided with the monster, turning him to stone.

'Whoa! COOOL!' Trip yelled.

'Nice teamwork, dude,' Zeke said, giving me a **FIST BUMP.**

'He's not going to be a statue for long,' Jez said. 'Not outside the glass cabinet. Let's get out of here while we can!'

We stepped over the monster
and hit the exit button, which was
now glowing blue because Jez had
hacked it unlocked.

The door **WHOOSHED OPEN.**

'Let's go!' Trip yelled.

We ran as fast as we could out
of the compound.

TUESDAY NIGHT

I opened my chat with Zeke.

Ari: My parents were so mad at me for being home late.

Zeke: Didn't they believe you about the monster?

Ari: Nope. They said I was playing a game. Wot about yours?

Zeke: Dad's seen weird stuff in portals cos of his army work.

Zeke: He's going to check it out tomorrow. But IDK if he believes me.

Ari: Lame.

Zeke: I'm smashed. C u @ school.

I shut down my computer and flopped onto my bed. What a day. I couldn't wait until everyone at school heard about how Jez, Zeke and I beat the monster!

WEDNESDAY MORNING

The bus rolled up at school and Zeke, Jez and I jumped out the doors. We saw a **BIG CROWD** of students standing in a circle.

'What's happening there?' Jez asked.

We walked over and saw Trip standing in the middle of the circle.

'And then I hacked the computer to open the doors. But the monster was guarding the door, so I had to do a **PARKOUR JUMP SPIN** and smash him in the head, then freeze him with his own club,' Trip said, waving his arms around.

'OOOOOH!' everyone gushed.

'That's not what happened! I hacked the computer!' Jez yelled.

'And Ari and I flattened the monster,' Zeke added.

Everyone turned and eyed us doubtfully. I looked Trip directly in the eyes. We'd saved his life. How could he act like this now?

But Trip glanced at the crowd. 'Do you avatars seriously believe those **NOOBS** saved me?' he laughed.

Everyone around him laughed and turned back to his story.

'What a **BLOCKHEAD,**' Zeke muttered.

'Who cares anyway,' I said, putting

my arms around my friends'
shoulders. 'We know the truth.'

'I thought you wanted to show him
that you were the bravest,' Zeke
said. 'A pro.'

I shrugged. 'I don't care what he
thinks. I don't need to prove myself
to him or anyone. And anyhow,'
I said, looking from Zeke to Jez,
'the reason we got out of there
alive wasn't because I was brave
or Zeke is an obby king or Jez is
a tech whiz. It was all of those
things. We're a **PRO TEAM.**'

Zeke's watch pinged.

'Whoa,' he said quietly.

'What is it?' Jez asked, leaning in.

'It's a message from my dad.
The army guys checked the
warehouse,' he said.

'Was the monster still there?' I asked.

Zeke shook his head. 'It's not just the monster that was gone. They said there was **NOTHING** in the warehouse at all.'

'No computers?' Jez asked.

'No computers. No automatic doors, no glass cabinet, no cupboards, no buttons, no . . . no nothing!' Zeke said.

We stared at each other with wide, disbelieving eyes.

'Dad says that was a stupid prank to pull on the army,' Zeke said, swallowing.

I couldn't believe it. How did the monster just disappear like that?

'Maybe it went through a **PORTAL?**' Jez said.

If it had been yesterday morning, I would have laughed at her. I barely even believed in portals. But after what we'd just gone through in that abandoned warehouse, I realised Blockville was a much **WEIRDER** place than I had ever known.

ANYTHING could happen.